Artwork © Pauline Burbidge
Authors: Judith Duffey Harding, Jennifer
Harris and Penny McMorris
Series Editor: Matthew Koumis
Graphic Design: Rachael Dadd & MK
Reprographics: Ermanno Beverari
Printed in Italy

© Telos Art Publishing 2004

Telos Art Publishing
1 Highland Square
Bristol BS8 2YB
England
t/f: +44 (0) 117 923 9124
e: editorial@telos.net
e: sales@telos.net
w: www.telos.net

ISBN 1 902015 71 1 (softback)

A CIP catalogue record for this book
is available from The British Library

Notes
All dimensions are shown in imperial and
metric, height x width. All work is in
private collections unless otherwise
stated. Place names are in the United
Kingdom unless otherwise indicated.

Photo Credits
All photography by Keith Tidball

Artist's Acknowledgements
To the anonymous American donor
without whom this book or my 'Quiltworks'
Exhibition would not have materialized.
I am most grateful for your generosity.
With many thanks to Keith Tidball for
doing such a great job, as always, with
these photographs. A big thank you to
the three authors, Penny McMorris,
Jennifer Harris and Judith Duffey Harding
for your expertise, help, encouragement
and enthusiasm. And of course to my
husband, Charlie Poulsen, who is always
very supportive.

Publisher's Acknowledgements
Thanks to Paul Richardson at Oxford
Brookes University; John Denison, Rosie
Tatham and Rosy Fowler.

Illustration on front cover:
The Waterfall (detail)
2003
fine cottons and silks collaged, pleated,
painted, stitched and quilted
78 x 82in (195 x 205cm)

Illustration back cover:
Intercut Fish Harmony (detail)
1991
fabric collage stiched and quilted
79 x 79in (200 x 200cm)
Textile Collection of the
Glasgow Museums

Illustration on pages 1 & 48:
Paxton Study I (detail)
1997
fabric collage, stitched and quilted
50 x 50in (127 x 127cm)
Collection of Angela Chisholm

portfolio collection
Pauline Burbidge

TELOS

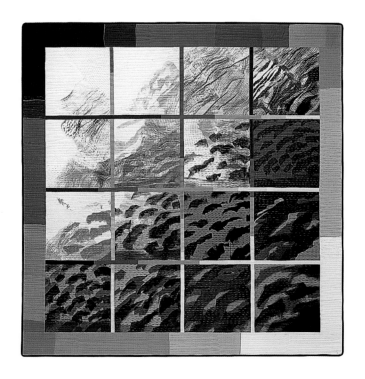

Contents

6   Foreword
          Jennifer Harris

11   Quiltmaking in an Age of Mechanical Inspiration:
          New work by Pauline Burbidge
          Judith Duffey Harding

27   Colour Plates

42   Biography

Wind Over Water
2003
fine cottons and silks, pleated,
painted, stitched and quilted
77 x 77in (195 x 195cm)

Foreword by Jennifer Harris

Dancing Lines
(detail; whole work illus. p 30)
1998
fabric collage,
stitched and quilted
78 x 78in (203 x 203cm)
Collection of the National
Museums of Scotland

Pauline Burbidge's most recent work is a revelation. In *The Waterfall*, one of the key pieces in her new series of black, white and grey 'quiltworks', she abandons the safety-net of the grid and the block, those underlying structures of the quilt canon which have been the hallmark of her work for more than two decades, and dips a brave toe into the unknown waters of work which no longer visually references quilt history or traditions. It is a huge step for an artist whose approach might be characterised as revolution through evolution.

And yet, on reflection, those who have followed Burbidge's career closely might not find this latest move towards structurally freer, more expressive work quite so unexpected as it first appears, for she has never ceased to push herself and to develop as an artist, albeit slowly and often imperceptibly, as nature itself evolves.

Her continual reinvention and regeneration of quilt traditions have made Burbidge an important catalyst in the development of the art quilt in both the UK and the USA, and work from every stage of her career is represented in major public and private collections. In the mid-1980s the precise geometry, meticulous piecing and optical dynamics of the American-style block quilts with which she first established her reputation were succeeded by more fluid and spontaneous image-making as, inspired by experiments with torn paper collage, she began to collage rather than piece fabric. Further innovations involved the deconstruction of the imagery within the blocks through 'intercutting' and the fracturing of images reflected in water, but her work remained anchored to the disciplined framework of the grid and the use of multiple, if no longer repeated, blocks.

Burbidge abandoned long ago the use of paper designs and templates as her image-making became more emotional and intuitive, though she has always taken photographs and made sketches. But these new landscapes are far less closely related to any visual source material than any of her previous work; they are, rather, a response to the natural world, an attempt to capture the spirit of place rather than its topography. Burbidge's work demonstrates above all the creative potential of process as a means of understanding for the artist and of communicating these discoveries to the viewer. Her unique visual language, based on supreme mastery of technique and handling of fabric, and the way she 'sees' a landscape in terms of colour, pattern and texture, have facilitated the most recent creative leap to the lyricism of her new work.

Burbidge's work lays no claim to any freighting with political or ideological issues. In a period when the art of the avant garde has been largely concept-driven, she has unashamedly privileged the aesthetic response of the viewer over ideas and meaning. Her work is an affirmation of the particular qualities of textile and the seductive effects of colour, even in this new monochrome series, which explores the subtlety of the whole range of shades between black and white. She may have begun to slip her moorings from the relative safety of the quilt harbour, but her work requires no new label for art, design and craft skills all interact in an electric way in this exciting new series.

Jennifer Harris
Deputy Director, Curator of Textiles,
The Whitworth Art Gallery,
University of Manchester, England

The Waterfall
2003
fine cottons and silks,
collaged, pleated, painted,
stitched and quilted
78 x 82in (195 x 205cm)

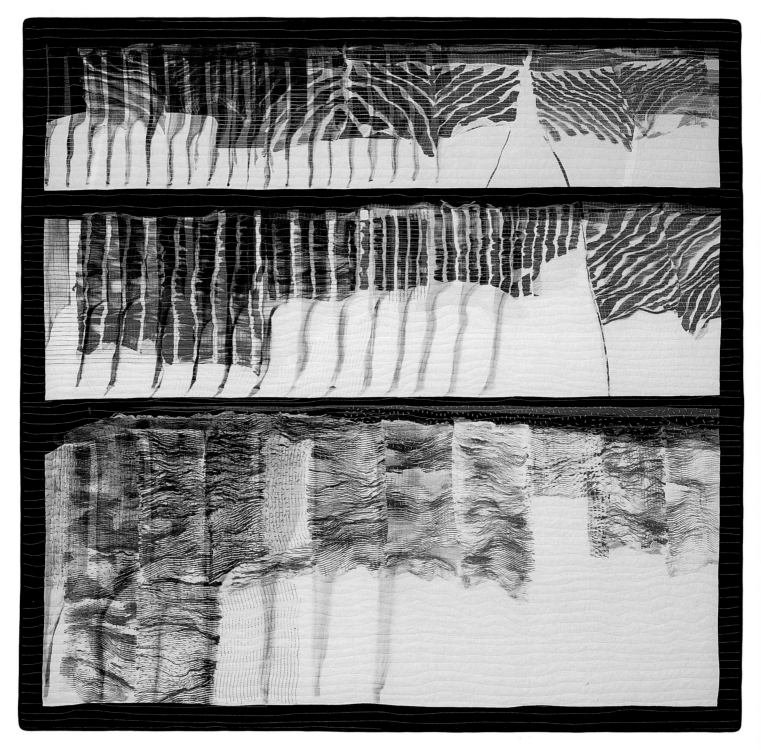

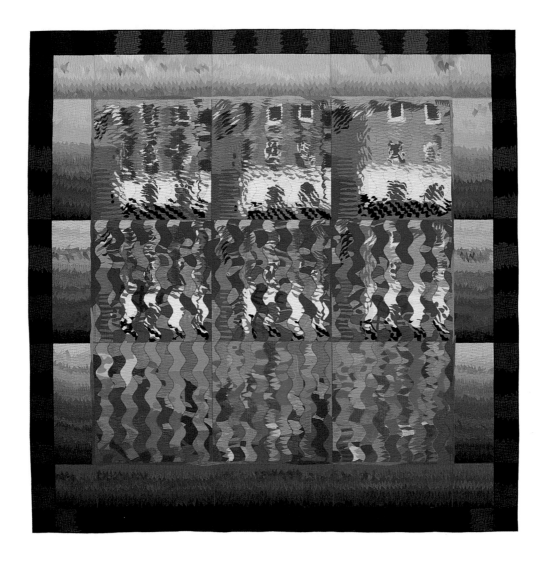

Quiltmaking in an Age of Mechanical Inspiration

New work by Pauline Burbidge

Judith Duffey Harding

Since her chance discovery in a junk shop of an old book on quilting prompted fashion/textile designer Pauline Burbidge to attempt her first quilt in 1975, her developing work has been marked by a consistent commitment to the possibilities and pleasures of this traditional form as an expressive contemporary medium. These solutions, however, have been realised in quite different ways.

Over her career, each exploratory step has seemed to cue another. Initial experiments with strip quilting, using natural forms as narrative starting points (as in the early heron and duck quilts), exploited the strong graphic potential inherent in the medium; nature submitted to the discipline of sewn geometry. These in turn led to further play with disciplined variations on familiar quilt blocks and patterns. Mirror-reflections of stairstep models introduced imagery based on architecture in larger, brightly coloured formats. As wider exploration of forms and subjects led

her to explore spontaneous torn-paper collages as preparatory work, direct cutting and design with freely cut, bonded and stitched fabric, took on a new role. She 'drew' with scissors. Hard-edged precision in lively arrangements played against controlled networks of stitching.

In a subsequent series of monumental quilts in the 90's based on water reflections, developed from photo studies, nature became her subject. This was due partly to her move from Nottingham with her husband, sculptor Charles Poulsen, to the wilder landscape of the Scottish Borders. Eager to explore and document her new environment, she wanted to capture in her work her delight in these intense experiences of her new personal surroundings. Natural forms and processes became subject and focus within the large scale quilts that maintained their characteristic strength of colour and bold, subtly varied patterning, anchored by strong solid borders.

page 10 and right:
Nottingham Reflections
1994
cotton fabric collage
stitched and quilted
82 x 82in (205 x 205cm)
Collection of
John M Walsh III

Feather Collection II

2003

cotton and silk fabrics,
feathers, paint, handstitching
and quilting

83 x 83in (206 x 206cm)

Anyone familiar with the impact of her vibrantly graphic style, widely recognised (and widely imitated), might be astonished to encounter her newest body of work produced over the last two years. Dramatic changes in outlook and execution have given the work a very different character. The dazzling primary contrasts have vanished, making way for complex and subtly evocative arrangements in black, white and grey. Far more restrained, contemplative in mood and almost sculptural, their newly irregular surfaces begin to disrupt the pictorial flatness of solid fabric. The bright graphic images her audiences might have expected have given way to a textural, painterly treatment.

What has changed and why? What has shaped this dramatic shift and how does its producer describe her newest investigations? And how do they relate to her earlier work?

Looking more closely at this new body of work, we see that, despite the immediate shock of the new, there is much that links reassuringly, if less explicitly, with earlier concerns. In *Feather Collections I and II*, which might be seen as transitional, the square grids still dominate, as does the notion of displaying natural objects through transparent layers. The gradual diagonal sweep from upper left to lower right still serves as an organising principle. Here, distinct, carefully chosen trios of patterned grey and white feathers, peer inquisitively out from stitched frames, asserting the range of decorative delight available in nature if only we take the time to look carefully. They suggest also the rich potential of a more limited palette. Here, she says, aware of imminent shifts, she was 'limbering up' for the work to come.

This delicacy of natural decoration is anticipated in the slightly earlier *Wind over Water* (page 4), a 16-square improvisation on the theme of subtly contrasting colour greys. Feathery rippling marks and free brush strokes hover like flocks of birds or floating leaves fluttering gently across the surface, capturing the counterpoint of simultaneous rhythms of flow and flight.

Such contrasts grow more dramatic in the *Waterfall* quilts, where the gentle reflective surface of a quiet stream gives way to the powerful crash of falling water, finally dissolving in white mist. Here the tension between the eerie silence before the moment of sudden breaking over rock is effectively conveyed by the broad sweep of cloth. No longer caught in a framework of square divisions, its movement is countered by multiple variations of rippling patterns painted on layers of transparent silks and voiles. The surfaces themselves seem to move. The pleated layers roll across the surfaces, playing against a thunder of dominant freely-painted black shapes. These quilts are almost audible, at once lyrical and loud, harmonious and dissonant, recreating the experience of observation of the force of water, of the tension between its movement and stillness.

That this evocative new strand in her work is the most naturalistic and descriptive yet, is all the more surprising when we learn that much of the specific form of its visual invention was due in part to another chance discovery: a new version of an old-fashioned 24-needle hand-pleating machine. She was drawn to this device at London's 'Knitting & Stitching Show' where her earlier work was on display. Intrigued by its use by embroiderers, she saw immediately its possibilities for her own purposes.

**Photo studies for
Wind Over Water**
2002
digital photos
7 x 7in (18 x 18cm) each photo

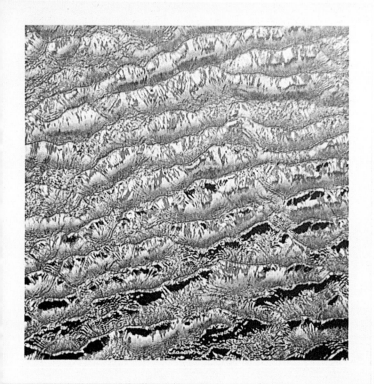
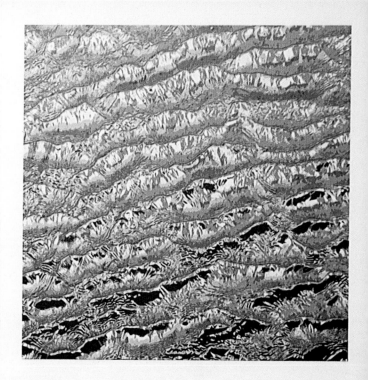
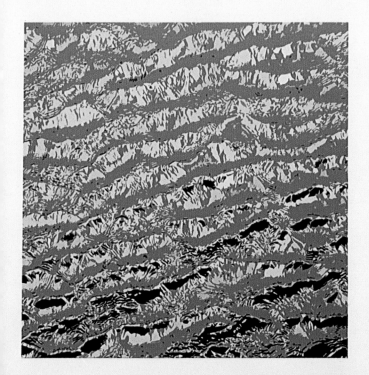

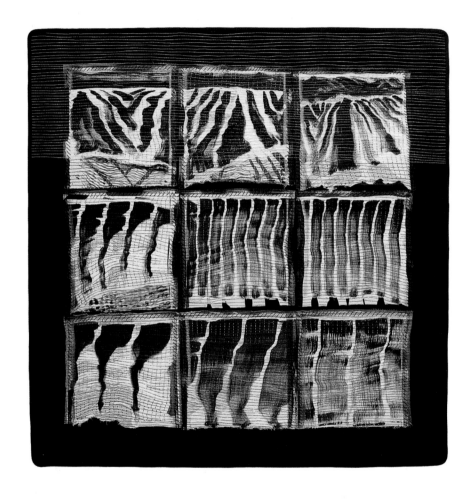

Climbing the Waterfall

2003

fine cotton fabrics, collaged, painted, pleated, stitched and quilted

38 x 38in (97 x 97cm)

Because the hand-pleating machine can only accommodate narrow lengths of lightweight fabric, she experimented with painting the edges of multiply-folded, thread-drawn, narrow bundles of thin fabric. These adventures coincided with an impulse to greater use of layered transparent patterns to capture the sense of overlapping, intersecting water patterns documented in her computer-manipulated photographic studies. These led in turn to further experiments with fine fabrics. The pleated fan-like layers, whose painted edges open out into intricate surface patterns, play against twisting, folded (but flexible) stacks of fabric that stream decoratively across the surface. Punctuation by a further layer of bold hand-stitching reinforces the contrasts. By imaginatively exploiting the possibilities of a 'new' mechanical device, she has been able to find

exactly the method and material to evoke the observations documented in her drawings and photos. To understand and exploit new possibilities for a new purpose seems one real key to invention.

Mechanical devices have always played an important role in her work with a medium that was, in tradition, valued as a product of hand crafting. Its slow, meditative rhythm measured out and ordered time and experience in terms of tiny, even stitches. Paradoxically, traditional judging of quilting technique often seemed to value hand-stitching insofar as it imitated machine-like qualities: 'tiny, regular, even stitches' were a mark of quality; while the freely exuberant stitching often found in quilts from other cultures, was often dismissed as clumsy and incompetent.[1]

Always quick to take advantage of relevant technology and mechanical innovation, whether domestic sewing or industrial quilting machines, digital cameras, or computer-generated images, Pauline Burbidge has enlivened tradition by embracing the new. Rows of functional machine stitching, initially hidden in the seams, gradually emerged, moving to the surface as bold decorative counterpoints to pieced and collaged fabric. Structurally, industrial quilting machines working in overall repetitive patterns pulled collaged surfaces together in coherent, solid wholes. Free arm machines have allowed a greater freedom to draw with stitch; spontaneous scribbling over a large surface becomes possible. (And it does not escape her notice that computer images, enlarged, echo the orderly fragmentation of traditional patchwork squares.) Similarly, the pleating machine has offered a technical means for dramatic change in the sculptural structure and painterly appearance of her most recent work.

Yet, though outward appearance may shift, the underlying concerns that make all these developments possible remain constant. Her love of fabric is primary and absolute. She immerses herself in it as a medium, engaging in the dialogue of hand and eye to find new ways of visually replicating intense responses to her natural surroundings. She speaks of 'wallowing in the experience of fabric', arguing that the work could only have been realised in this medium, not any other. It offers the flexible, fluid language that grounds the imagery she documents and urges us to share.

The physical process of making is equally important. Making becomes a kind of meditation. A still 'wordless space' follows the active 'busy-ness' of preparatory work. Here the connections, seen and sensed, are realised. Like the focussed immersing of herself in observation and recording of natural phenomena, the making allows a distillation of those connections in what she describes as an 'almost spiritual' experience.

Intercut Fish Harmony (detail)
1991
fabric collage stiched and quilted
79 x 79in (200 x 200cm)
Textile Collection of the
Glasgow Museums

pages 22 & 25:

Horizon

2003

fine cotton and silks, pleated,
collaged, stitched and quilted
80 x 81in (205 x 207cm)

Horizon perhaps explains this best, with silent visual eloquence. Here is the still meeting point of action and contemplation, the resolution where sky and earth both rest, meeting in final agreement. There is fulfilment but quiet sadness in this image of finality, like the moment of completion when the last stitch signals not only the end of a piece of work, but also the cutting off of paths to further possibilities. New journeys begin.

Teaching internationally has always played a central role in Burbidge's life. While she has welcomed the chance to reflect on the responsibilities of teaching as well as thinking about the process of quiltmaking from different perspectives, it has also occupied an enormous amount of time. She has been a popular and effective teacher, through her books and workshops, but balancing this with her own work has not been easy. Though she very much enjoys the people and the activity, she is also concerned by the questions teaching raises of the value of skill and authority, the nature of artistic judgement, and the difficulties of dealing with questions that may have no real answer apart from the inquiry of exploration itself. It can also be discouraging to work with the few audiences who look for instant solutions and easy answers, and who may find it difficult to take their own work seriously. So when the possibility of a period of sponsorship enabled her to concentrate solely on the development of her new work, she was grateful for her first real breathing space in twenty years. In developing this new body of work, she has valued the space to grapple with the more personal issue of her own learning from and through a challenging medium.

In all her work, but perhaps especially in this most recent collection, Pauline Burbidge has pioneered the inventive revival of the quilt form as an artistic medium. It expresses a personal vision that resonates with her own feeling for her constantly changing environment. There are pioneer echoes too in her reclaiming, with diligence, discomfort and hard work, her current living and working space from challenging beginnings. In a single-minded commitment to a vernacular form, she avoids the tangle of theoretical discussions of the place of her medium in the complex nested hierarchies of fine art and craft, or the relationships of the varied 'artworlds' identified within quilting culture.[2] Whether her activity falls into the 'holistic' or 'prescriptive' distinctions that make the quilt as a form a complex, politically loaded, gendered commodity rather than a creative process full of inventive promise, is irrelevant.[3] It is the making that matters.

In terms of her work, the word 'quilt' seems more a verb than a noun, a sequence of seeing and responding, rather than an object. Though she might readily accept and value the form's tradition and associations, she chooses not to engage in the more intricate discussions of the complex status of quilting; she tries to keep an accessible perspective. Balancing delicately somewhere on the multiple boundaries between fine art, high craft, personal diary and domestic document, this medium is, for her, not just a means, but the means of realising a personal vision. This is accomplished through the fabric medium that she has helped to develop and dignify, of which she has intimate knowledge, profound feeling and sensitive control. She calls them 'quiltworks' with all the historical and technical evocations these words bear; these quilts do, indeed, 'work' in every sense.

It has been argued that the activity of quiltmaking is essentially about ways of ordering, of materials, of processes, of lives. In Pauline Burbidge's new work, a traditional medium, using mechanical means of ordering as inspiration, becomes a unique way of making perceptions visible. The fleeting wonder of nature in action can be caught and shown; restrictions, once more, lead to new freedoms.

Dr. Judith Duffey Harding
Art Historian and Sculptor
University Teaching Fellow,
Middlesex University, England

Notes
1. Susan Behuniak-Long, 'Preserving the Social Fabric: Quilting in a technological World', *Quilt Culture, Tracing the Pattern*, ed. Cheryl Torsney and Judy Elsely, Columbia, London, University of Missouri Press, 1994
2. Susan E. Bernick, 'A quilt is an art object when it stands up like a man', Torsney and Elsely, 1994
3. Behuniak-Long, op.cit

Colour Plates

Whiteadder
1995
collaged cotton fabrics,
lamination, plastic and stitching
33 x 33in (83 x 83cm)
Collection of Claire Crocker & Adam Lury

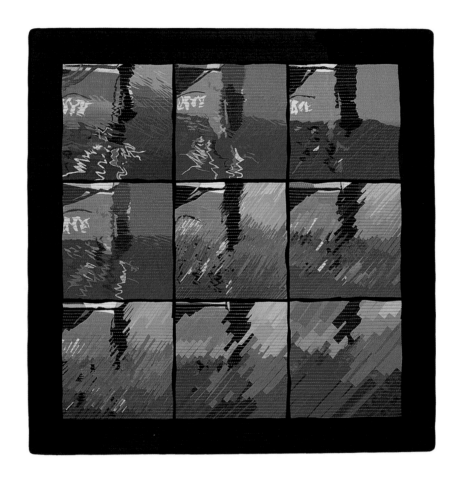

Pittenweem Quilt

2002

fabric collaged, stitched and quilted

59 x 59in (150 x 150cm)

right:

Black and White Feathers

1996

cotton fabric, feathers,

laminating plastic, stitching

and quilting

15 x 21in (38 x 53cm)

page 30:

Dancing Lines

1998

fabric collaged, stitched

and quilted

80 x 80in (203 x 203cm)

Collection of the National

Museums of Scotland

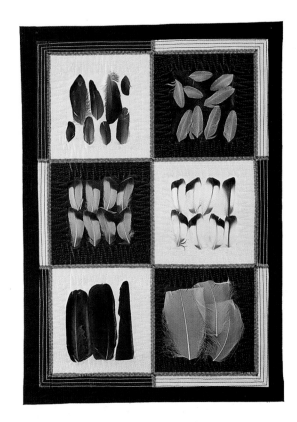

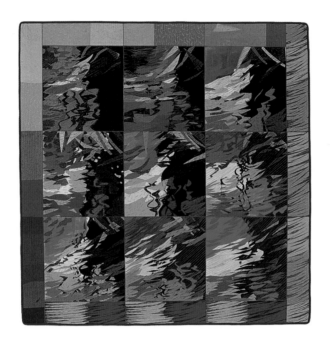

above:

Paxton Study I

1997

fabric collage, stitched and quilted

50 x 50in (127 x 127cm)

Collection of Angela Chisholm

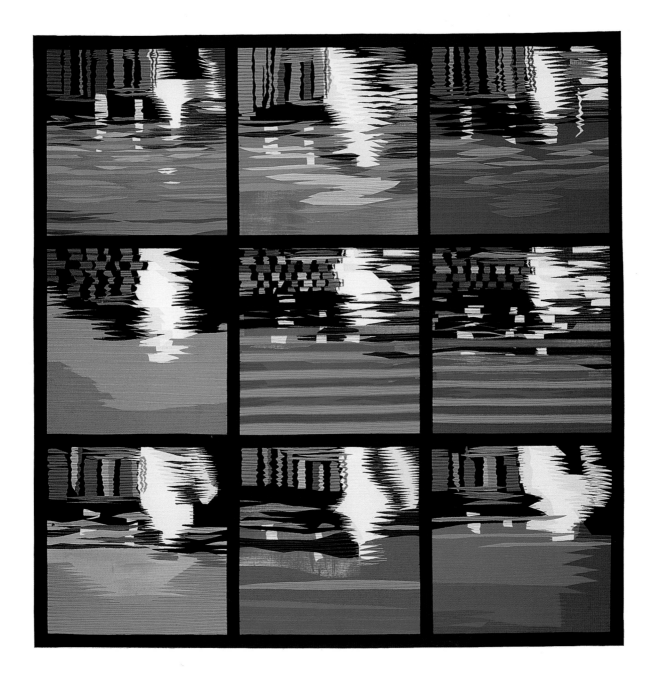

page 33 & left:
Tweed Reflections II
1995
fabric collage,
stitched and quilted
48 x 48in (121 x 121cm)
Collection of John M Walsh III

page 36 (detail; whole work illus. p18)
Climbing the Waterfall
2003
fine cotton fabrics, collaged,
painted, pleated, stitched
and quilted
38 x 38in (97 x 97cm)

page 38 & 39:
Honesty Quilt
2003
cotton fabric, honesty seeds, laminating
plastic, stitching and quilting
76 x 75in (192 x 190cm)

pages 37, 40 & 41 (details; whole work illus. p9)
The Waterfall
2003
fine cottons and silks collaged, pleated,
painted, stitched and quilted
78 x 82in (195 x 205cm)

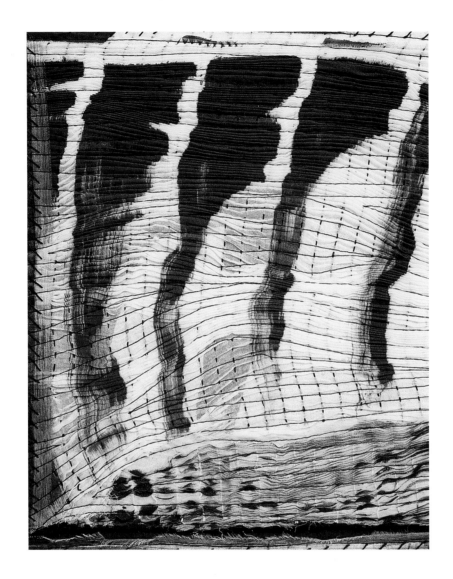

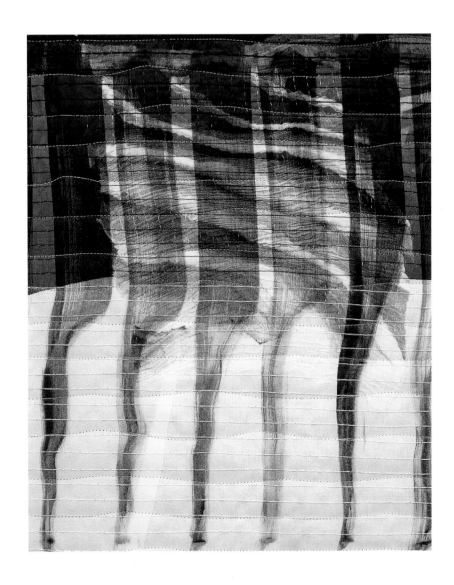

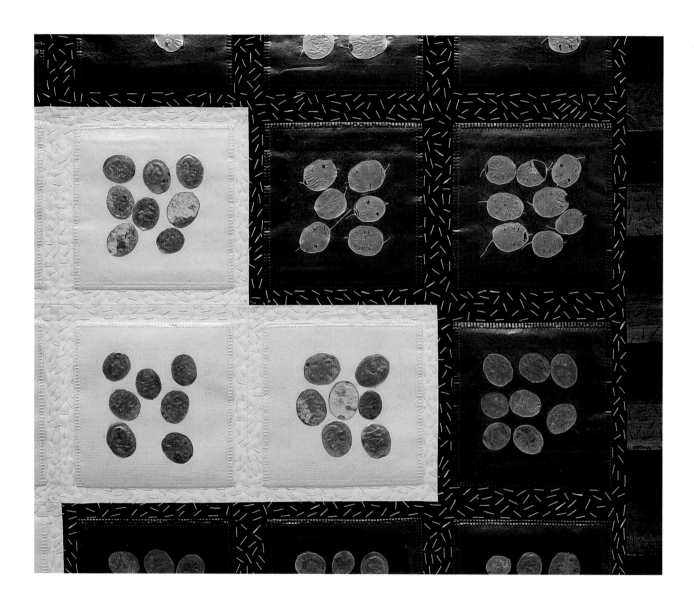

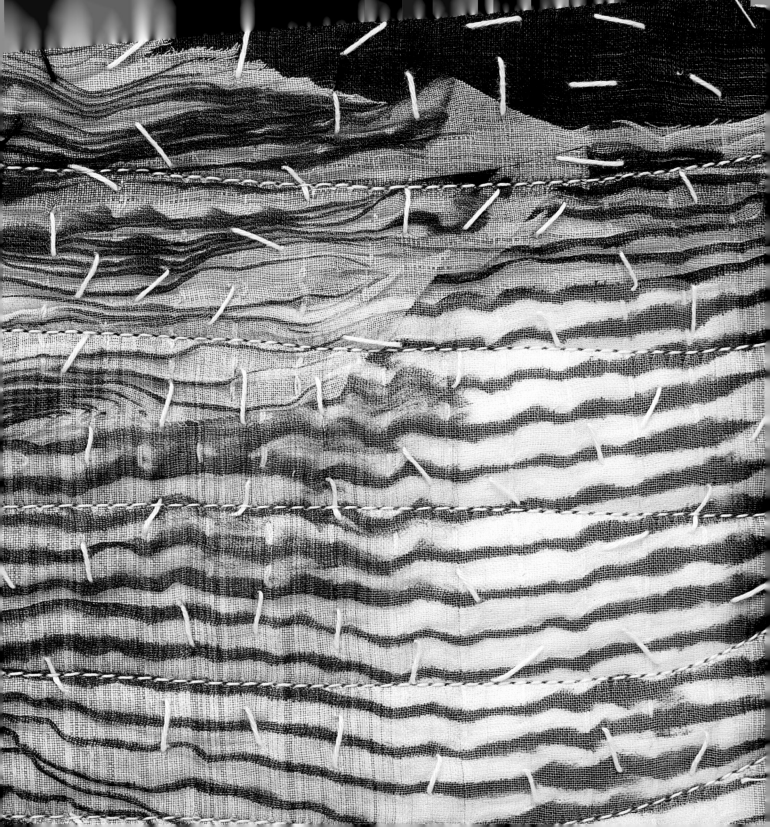

Biography

Born   1950, Dorset, UK

Education
1967–69   Pre-Diploma, Art & Design, Yeovil Technical College
1969–70   Diploma, London College of Fashion
1970–73   Dip AD Fashion / Textiles, St. Martin's School of Art, London

Awards
1996   The Scottish Arts Council
1982   John Ruskin Award
1978   New Craftsman's Grant, Crafts Council, London

Solo Exhibitions
2004–05   'QUILTWORKS'. The Shipley Art Gallery, Gateshead;
                               tour: The Knitting & Stitching Show, London, Dublin & Harrogate;
                               Canterbury Royal Museum and Art Gallery, Canterbury;
                               The Collins Gallery, Glasgow; Bankfield Museum, Halifax
2000   'European Patchwork Meeting', Sainte Marie-aux-Mines, Alsace, France
1991   'Pauline Burbidge', The Works Gallery, Philadelphia, USA
1989   'Pauline Burbidge', The Ruskin Craft Gallery, Sheffield
1983   'New Patchwork Quilt', Midland Group, Nottingham
1979   'Quilts by Pauline Burbidge', Foyles Art Gallery, London

right: page 45 (detail; whole work illus. p5)
Feather Collection I (detail)   **Wind Over Water**
2003   2003
cotton and silk fabrics, feathers, paint,   fine cottons and silks, pleated,
handstitching and quilting   painted, stitched and quilted
43 x 43in (110 x 110cm)   77 x 77in (195 x 195cm)

Selected Group Exhibitions

2004	'LODZ '04: 11th International Triennial of Tapestry', Poland *(invited Artist)* (cat.)
2003	'30/30 Vision', Crafts Council, London (tour, catalogue)
	'OPEN STUDIO Exhibition', Allanton, Scottish Borders, UK
	(annual exhibition since 1994 with sculptor Charles Poulsen)
2002	'Contemporary Art Quilts', The John M. Walsh Collection,
	University of Kentucky Art Museum, USA (catalogue)
	'Visual Arts Scotland', OceanTerminal, Leith, Edinburgh *(invited Artist)*
2001	'Ground Cover: Contemporary Quilts', OWCC Arts Center Galleries,
	Niceville, Florida, USA (catalogue)
2000-01	'British Contemporary Quilt Exhibition', Matsuzakaya Department Stores,
	Nagoya / Tokyo / Osaka, Japan
	'North Country Quilts: Legend & Living Tradition', Bowes Museum, Co. Durham (cat.)
1999	'Visual Arts Scotland', Royal Scottish Academy, Edinburgh *(invited Artist)*
1998–99	'Take 4 – New Perspectives on the British Art Quilt', The Whitworth Art Gallery,
	University of Manchester (tour, catalogue)
1995	'Raw Materials', Old Gala House, Galashiels (tour, catalogue)
1994	'Quilts with Conviction', Hove Museum & Art Gallery, Hove, UK
1993	'Joining Forces', Angel Row Gallery, Nottingham (tour)
	(two-person exhibition with sculptor Charles Poulsen)
1993, 1991, 1987, 1985	'Quilt National', The Dairy Barn, Athens, Ohio (tour, catalogues)
1992	'New Wave Quilt Collections II' (tour, catalogue)
	'Quilts Now', Zephyr Gallery, Louisville, KY, USA
1991	'Eleven Contemporary Quiltmakers', One Mellon Center, Pittsburgh, USA,
1990	'Contemporary English Design', Sheehan Gallery, Whitman College,
	Washington, USA (catalogue)
1987	Contemporary Textile Gallery, London, UK
	'Wall to Wall', The Cornerhouse, Manchester (tour, catalogue)

Public Collections

Aberdeen Art Gallery, Aberdeen
National Museums of Scotland, Edinburgh
Museum of Costume and Textiles, Nottingham
The Glasgow Museums, Glasgow
The Whitworth Art Gallery, University of Manchester
The Victoria & Albert Museum, London
The Shipley Art Gallery, Gateshead
The Ruskin Gallery, Sheffield
The Ulster Folk Museum, Belfast
The Crafts Council, London
The James Collection, International Quilt Study Center, University of Nebraska, USA
The Collection of John M. Walsh III, New Jersey, USA

Selected Commissions

1994	'Nottingham Reflections', John M. Walsh III, USA
1990	'Striped Canopy' & 'Canopy II', Nottingham County Council, for Mansfield Arts Centre, UK
1988	'Ship Shape', The Benjamin Britten High School, Lowestoft, UK

Professional

2003	Studio Workshops, Allanton, Scottish Borders, UK (annually since 1994)
2002	Lecturer, Victoria & Albert Museum, 'Art of the Stitch' Study Days
1997	Quilt Week Yokohama – Design classes (tour)
1996	Quilt Surface Design Symposium, Columbus, Ohio, USA
1995	Split Rock Arts Program, University of Minnesota, USA
1993	'Mainstream Design Conference', St John's, Newfoundland (Tutor & Speaker)
1993	Co-selector for 'Contemporary American Quilts', a Crafts Council exhibition, London
1989	The Crafts Council Committee, London
1986 / 87	Setting-Up Grants Committee, Crafts Council, London
1985	Founder Member of 'Quilt Art', UK
1979	Founder Member of The Quilters' Guild, UK

Selected Bibliography

2003	Ichikawa, Naomi. 'Pauline Burbidge', *Patchwork Quilt Tsushin* magazine, Japan, June (no. 114)
2003	'30/30 Vision', exh. cat. Crafts Council, London
2002	Longville, Tim/Corbett, Val. 'In living colour', *Caledonia* magazine, UK, November
2001	'The nineties collection', exh. cat. The Quilters' Guild of the British Isles
2001	'Ground cover: contemporary quilts', exh. cat. O.W.C.C. Arts Center Galleries, Niceville, Florida, USA
2001	'Contemporary art quilts', exh. cat. The John M. Walsh Collection, University of Kentucky Art Museum, USA,
2000	Osler, Dorothy. 'North country quilts: legend & living tradition', exh. cat. Bowes Museum, UK
2000	Burbidge, Pauline. *Quiltstudio*, The Quilt Digest Press USA [now McGraw-Hill]
1998	Shaw, Robert. *The Art Quilt*, Hugh Lauter Levin Associates, USA
	'TAKE 4 – new perspectives on the British art quilt', exh. cat. The Whitworth Art Gallery, University of Manchester; & Telos Art Publishing, UK
1997	James, Michael. 'Reflections of a career at midstream', *Art / Quilt Magazine* USA, issue 7
1995	'88 leaders in the quilt world today', *Nihon Vogue*, Japan
1992	Lintott, Pam/Miller, Rosemary. *The Quilt Room*, Letts, UK
1991	Duffey, Judith. 'A gentler geometry', *Crafts* magazine, UK, Nov/Dec
1990	Walker, Michelle. *The Passionate Quilter*, Ebury Press, UK
1990	Barker, Vicki/Bird, Tessa. *The Fine Art of Quilting*, Studio Vista, UK
1987	'Pieced pictures', three programmes for Channel 4 television
1987	Holmes, Madeline/Ledger, Chris. 'Industrial revolution', Video, AVA Nottingham, UK
1986	McMorris, Penny/Kile, Michael. 'The art quilt', catalogue, The Quilt Digest Press, USA
1981	Burbidge, Pauline. *Making Patchwork for Pleasure & Profit*, John Gifford Ltd, UK
1980	Nuemark, Victoria. 'Quilts by Pauline Burbidge'. *Crafts* magazine, UK, May/June,